What Makes a Giraffe Laugh?

Animal Poems

Written by Michael Beadle
Illustrated by Arianne Hemlein

Michael Beadle

What Makes a Giraffe Laugh / written by Michael Beadle;
illustrated by Arianne Hemlein
ISBN 9781667838182

Published by BookBaby
7905 N. Crescent Blvd. Pennsauken, NJ. 08110

This book is dedicated to all the amazing students,
teachers and poets who have inspired me over the years
and to my wife, Diane,
for all your love, patience and support.

-Michael Beadle

To Kelsey and Cooper for all of the precious hours
spent reading beautiful picture books together and to
my sisters for their enduring support of my dreams.

-Arianne Hemlein

Table of Contents

Frog Song

Let's hop today.
      Let's flop today.
Let's leap and stop
      and splop today.

Let's splish today.
      Let's splash today
on pads and fronds
      and ponds today.

Let's sing today.
      Let's dance away.
Let's wiggle and squiggle
      and giggle today.

Let's dream today
      in the stream today,
in the wet and the wild
      of the world today.

Picklebug, Ticklebug

Picklebug, ticklebug
Tiny little toes

Noodlebug, doodlebug
Fuzzy little clothes

Wigglebug, jigglebug
Inching up a tree

Needlebug, skeedlebug
Looking down at me

Ants Won't Dance

Ants won't dance,
Not in India, China or France.
You could put them in a trance
Or read them verses of romance,
But you won't get a single one to slow dance.
You could offer them free lessons to tap dance
Or square dance or line dance
Or breakdance in sweatpants,
But they just won't dance.
And even if you had an army of ants
In a jungle full of plants,
You'd never get the chance
To watch any of them so much as prance
Because   ants   simply   won't   dance.

Tell Me

Hello, beetle—
      Hello, ant—
Tell me, what's your favorite plant?

Hello, spider—
      Hello, fly—
Where do you go when you want to hide?

Hello, cricket—
      Hello, moth—
Are you home or are you lost?

Hello, hornet—
      Hello, bee—
What's it like to live so free?

Welcome to the Woods

Welcome to the woods
of birch, oak and pine,
where chipmunks chatter
and squirrels climb.

Welcome to the woods
of hare and hawk,
where centipedes slither
in the shadow of a fox.

Welcome to the woods
where a silver creek wanders,
where the deer step softly,
and the barred owl ponders.

Welcome to the woods
of moss, log and limb,
where the bluebird of morning
sings a green, golden hymn.

Advice

Don't howl
at an owl.

Don't squawk
at a hawk.

Don't cackle
at a grackle.

Don't keep secrets
from egrets.

Don't feed carrots
to parrots.

Don't tease geese
with gourmet cheese.

Don't hide French fries
from a seagull's eyes.

Never tempt a pigeon—
not even a smidgeon.

And even in jest,
it's best not to test
the talons of a peregrine falcon.

Greetings

Hello, junko!
Cheerio, vireo!

Whad'ya know, Mr. Crow?
How's the weather, Miss Woodpecker?

Lookin' regal, Brother Eagle.
Wish you luck, Sister Duck.

Will it rain, Cousin Crane?
Maybe an inch, says Aunt Finch.

Enjoy the day, Miss Blue Jay.
See you again, Señor Wren.

So long, adieu and too-da-loo!
Glad to chat with each of you.

Gray Squirrel

once again
you tiptoe
the tight wire

dangle
at odd angles
crouch
to pounce

spread-eagle leap
from antlered branch
to leaf splash

scramble after
ample acorns
that will adorn
your secret stash
your glut of nuts

off you bound
kernel catcher
eager streaker
sneaky retreater

deftly climb
the gnarly oak
park on a perch
nook of a notch

to savor
that plump prize
between
your paws

Guesssssss Who?

Wormy squirmer
  Wiggly squiggler

        Viney climber
      Slender defender

      Green garter
    Desert darter

    Rattle shaker
  Venom maker

  Tree hugger
Jungle lover

Miss Hisser
  Mr. Slither

    Hyper viper
      Striped striker

        King cobra
          Whoa boa!

Birthday Wishes

I don't want an anaconda for my birthday;
Don't need a chimpanzee to bring me cake.
What I'd love is a hug from a panda
And a sky of fireflies across a lake.

You'll Never Catch Me

I'm walking in the wild woods
and what do I see?
A polka-dotted, yellow-spotted
bear in a tree!
Run bear, run bear,
run after me—
you can run all you want,
but you'll never catch me.

I'm swimming in a river
and what do I see?
A Talladega alligator
chomping after me!
Chomp gator, chomp gator,
chomp after me—
you can chomp all you want,
but you'll never catch me.

I'm sailing to an island
and what do I see?
A mama llama from Bahama
surfing after me!
Surf away, surf away,
surf after me—
you can surf all you want,
but you'll never catch me.

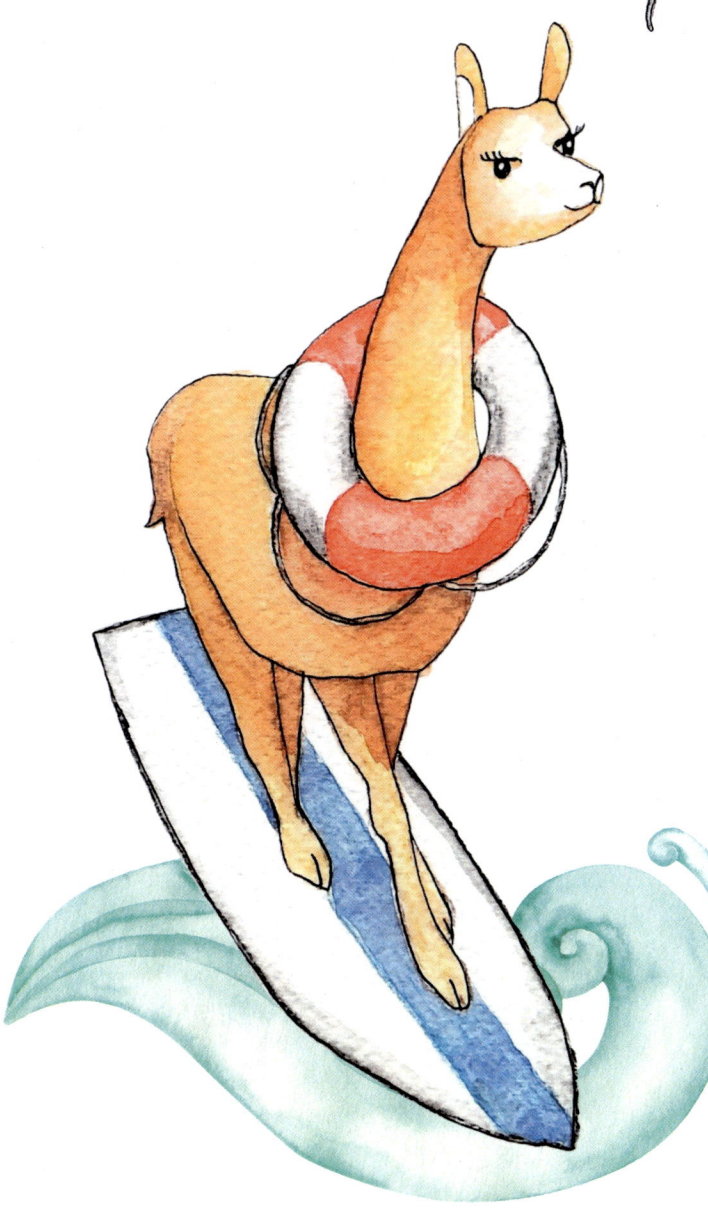

I'm floating in the ocean
and what do I see?
An albatross with dental floss
swooping after me!
Swoop bird, swoop bird,
swoop after me—
you can swoop all you want,
but you'll never catch me.

19

Alligator Café

What's that grumblin' in my tummy today?
I gotta wanna have some food right away.

I got the hungries, the munchies, so where's my next snack?
I think I'll go down across the railroad track.

I got a friend waitin' there; he knows just what to do.
He'll serve you up the best stew you ever knew.

He's the top chef here and for miles around.
He's got long rows of teeth, and he never wears a frown.

Oooooh, Alligator, Alligator, what's before lunch?
I think I wanna have that crackleberry crunch.

Alligator, Alligator, what's the déjeuner?
The red potato, two tomato soup of the day.

And Alligator, Alligator, what's for dessert?
A chocolate soufflé you can take back to work.

Oooooh, alligator, alligator, love your recipes.
Thanks again, my dear ol' friend; I'll see ya next week!

 déjeuner = [DAY-juh-NAY] French word for "lunch"

The Kitchen Thief

Inspector Raccoon
Is on the case:
A stolen pizza
No one can trace.

He's searched the lawn
And sifted through trash.
Someone got away
In a midnight dash.

It's all so sudden—
This feast of crimes.
Also gone missing
A sandwich of mine,

A box of cookies
And barbecue chips,
A hot apple pie
And queso dip.

I'm hoping to catch
This culprit red-handed.
He's sneaky and quick,
A keen-eyed bandit.

For weeks the Inspector
Has gathered up clues,
Tracks of small feet
Without any shoes.

Does he have a suspect?
Does he know who it is?
How strange the footprints
Look just like his.

What Makes a Giraffe Laugh?

What makes a giraffe laugh?
What advice would you offer mice?

What do lemurs dream
while they sit by a stream?

How would an alligator ride an escalator?

How many balloons
should you give a baboon?

What would an iguana say to a piranha?
Anything he'd wanna?

What would a kangaroo do
with eighteen pairs of tennis shoes?

What might an elephant invent
if given time and a ton of cement?

Where could I go
to watch a flamingo
play the piano in a limo?

I sure would like to know.

The Ocelot

The ocelot is hard to spot,
Even if you hide and squat
Behind thick vines and jungle rot.
You could wait and wait . . . and then what?
Perhaps you'd slumber on a warm cot
And dream of birds with polka dots
Or butterflies that can't be caught
Or bright red bowls of apricots;
And while you slept, out would trot
The rarest and fairest ocelot.

Footwear

Herons wear high heels.
Bison wear boots.
Marmots wear moccasins
With fuzzy suits.

Tigers wear tennis shoes.
Sloths wear slippers.
Seals wear silly socks
That slide on their flippers.

Lynxes wear loafers.
Cougars wear cleats.
I wonder what millipedes
Wear on their feet.

Animal Associations

Lions abide in prides.
Wolves will hunt in packs.
Lemurs crouch in conspiracies
Before they seek out snacks.

Whales prevail in pods.
Penguins prefer a colony.
Fish find bliss in schools
To study oceanography.

Porcupines meet in prickles.
Giraffes assemble in towers.
Owls convene a parliament
To hone their nightly powers.

Ferrets form a business.
Gorillas join a band.
Moles uphold their labor
In a little plot of land.

Slothability

Thoughtfully,
slothfully,
they savor slow time.

Curiously,
unhurriedly,
they cling like a vine.

Snuggling,
cuddling
in a hammock of fur,

they choose
to peruse
like a canopy connoisseur.

30

Their utopia
is cecropia,
high leaves in the mist,

or delicious
hibiscus:
a sloth snack sun-kissed.

Whether snoozing
or amusing
or slothing in a tree,

these creatures
are teachers
of dexterity.

Cecropia = [seh-CRO-pee-uh] a tropical tree
favored by three-toed sloths in Costa Rica

Newt in a Three-Piece Suit

A newt in a three-piece suit
Will avoid eating sweets or fruit.
He won't take chances
On staining his pantses.
Does that make him shy or astute?

Love Birds

Rudy the blue-footed booby
Fell in love with a seagull named Judy.
One day in the rain,
He called out her name,
And when she winked back, he thought, "Groovy!"

Arlo Stitch

My name is Arlo Stitch,
Best tailor of the sea.
I hem the finest dresses
For whale and manatee.

I fashion silken stockings
For squids and octopi,
Pink sarongs for dark dugongs,
A coat for a clam that's shy.

My clients can be picky
And often hard to please—
Just last week a school of fish
All wanted dungarees.

They tell me Arctic seals
Adore a fuzzy hat,
And urchins love a little lace—
I've no problem with that.

But some insist on woeful styles
I ardently reject.
I'll give a shark a brand-new scarf
But never a turtleneck.

The Dolphin

(with apologies to William Blake's "The Tyger")

Dolphin! Dolphin! leaping high,
Over waves that multiply.
What eternal force of motion
Keeps you bounding through the ocean?

With your skill of echolocation,
Where will you go for your next vacation?
And when you get there, what will you find?
A sunset beach? A pool to unwind?

What a way to see the world—
To splash and spin as waves unfurl.
To glimpse your graceful tail or fin
Makes my heart rejoice again.

Octopus

Here she comes—
　　an octopus,
　　　a rocktopus,
　　　an eight-armed soctopus.

A curlopus,
　a swirlopus
　　that turns and churns
　　　in front of us.

An inktopus,
　a slinktopus
　　that squirts and darts
　　　away from us.

O octopus,
　dear rocktopus,
　　please, o please
　　　come back to us!

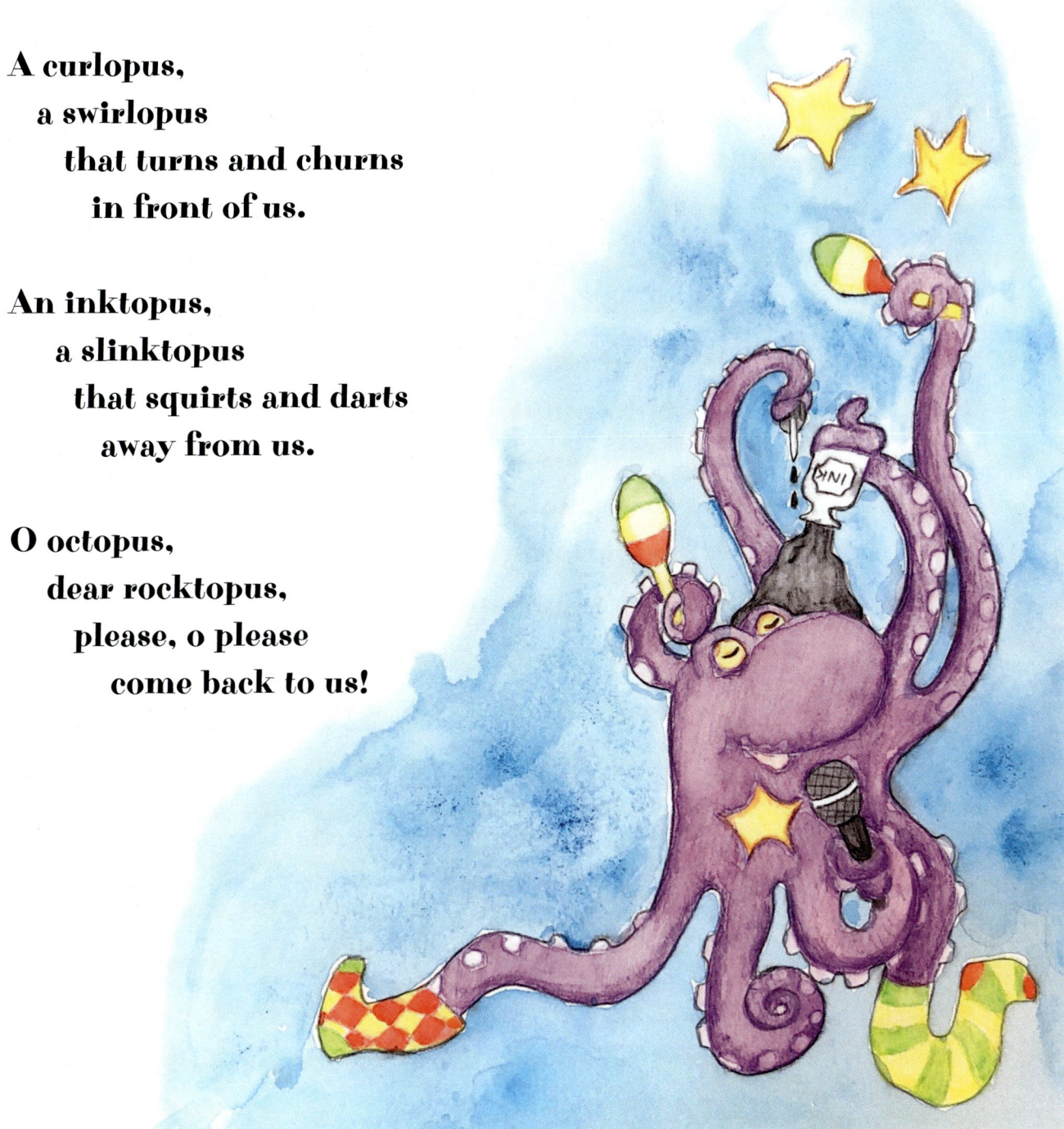

Shark Goes to the Dentist

Let's have another look
At all those pearly whites.
Open wide as I lean inside
And shine a little light.

Let's take another X-ray
And check for cavities.
This won't take long; your gums are strong—
Just please don't cough or sneeze.

I think your teeth look fine.
Excuse this metal scraper.
We'll rinse and freshen and finish this session.
I'll bill you for my labor.

I'd recommend some flossing—
You've got some plaque in places.
And to be honest, I'm no orthodontist,
But I think you need some braces.

Jellyfish

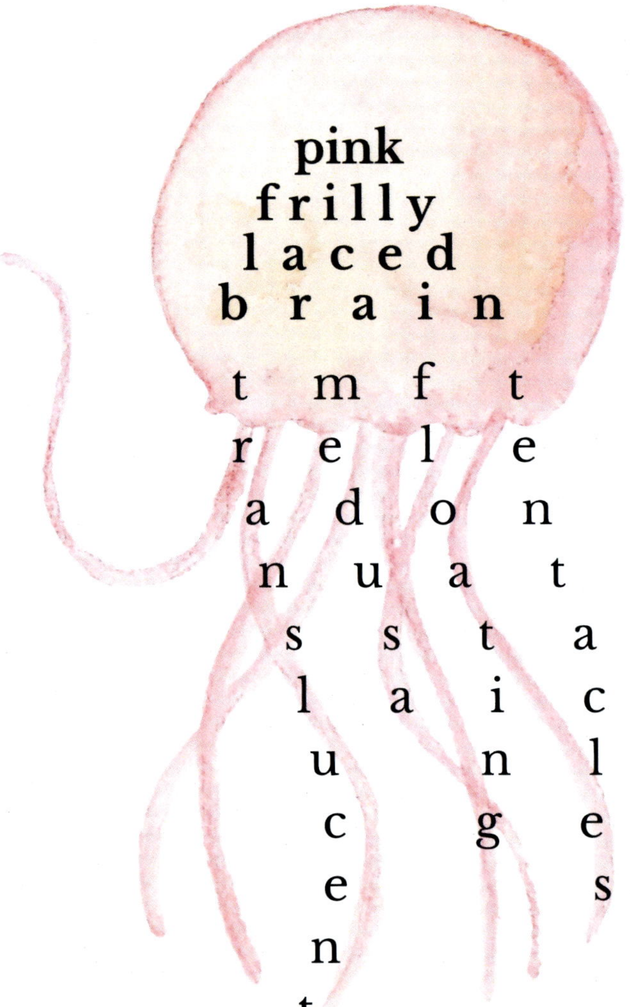

pink
frilly
laced
brain
t m f t
r e l e
a d o n
n u a t
s s t a
l a i c
u i n l
c n g e
e s
n
t

rosy
topaz
parachute
d e s
a l t
n e r
g c i
l t n
i r g
n i s
g f
i
e
d

40

aqua
marine
lampshade

i   d   d
l   a   e
l   r   p
u   k   t
m   e   h
i   s   s
n   t
a
t
i
n
g

This Blue Gigantic Sea
(with apologies to Emily Dickinson's "I Never Saw a Moor")

I never swam with sharks.
I never touched an eel.
But I know when a jelly stings
And how it makes you feel.

I never rode a seahorse.
I never held a whelk.
I only stepped on barnacles
And slipped on slimy kelp.

I never flew with flying squid
Or roared with lionfish,
But if I keep my fingers crossed,
I hope to get my wish.

I never saw the bottom
Of this blue gigantic sea,
But how I love the wondrous waves
That tumble back to me.

Author

Michael Beadle is a poet, author and writer-in-residence living in Raleigh, N.C. Since 1998, he's been performing and teaching poetry for students of all ages. A former journalist and high school English teacher, he's taught thousands of students and teachers as a writing instructor, visiting teaching artist, and A+ Schools Fellow. His poems have been featured in books, anthologies, literary journals, and the N.C. Zoo. His inspiration comes from all kinds of sources: hiking in the woods, teaching students, researching animal habitats, and reading the poetry of Jack Prelutsky, Douglas Florian, Joyce Sidman, Kristine O'Connell George, Eve Merriam, and many others.

Illustrator

Arianne Hemlein graduated with a B.A. in English from UNC. She has been making a living as an artist since 2009 in Cary, NC, painting murals in homes and businesses and creating portraiture, custom art, and illustration. She finds endless inspiration in nature and marvels at the way the whole world is reflected in a raindrop, the symphony of leaves rustled by a breeze, and the dance of tree shadows upon the ground. You can see her work on her website, www.designsbyarianne.com, or contact her by email at arianne.hemlein@gmail.com